Roping Can Be Hazardous To Your Health

ROPING CAN BE HAZARDOUS TO YOUR HEALTH

by Curt Brummett

illustrations by Wendell E. Hall

August House Publishers, Inc.

L I T T L E   R O C K

Published by August House, Inc.,
P.O. Box 3223, Little Rock, Arkansas, 72203,
501-372-5450.

Printed in the United States of America
10 9 8 7 6 5 4 3 2 1

LIBRARY OF CONGRESS CATALOGING-IN-PUBLICATION
DATA

Brummett, Curt
Roping can be hazardous to your health / by Curt Brummett : illustrations
by Wendell E. Hall. — 1st ed.
p.   cm.
ISBN 0-87483-146-6 (pb : alk. paper) : $6.95
1. Southwest, New—Social life and customs—Humor. 2. Cowboys—
Southwest, New—Humor. 3. Brummett, Curt—Childhood and
youth—Humor. I. Title.
F787.B77 1991
979—dc20   91-28007

First Edition, 1991

All these stories appeared first and in different form in *Livestock Weekly,*
Horse and Rider, DeBaca County News, Team Ropers Times, or in *My
Dog's a Democrat,* Maverick Books, 1985.

Executive: Liz Parkhurst
Project editor: Judith Faust
Cover design and illustrations: Wendell E. Hall
Typography: Lettergraphics, Little Rock

This book is printed on archival-quality paper which meets the
guidelines for performance and durability of the Committee on
Production Guidelines for Book Longevity of the
Council on Library Resources.

AUGUST HOUSE, INC.   PUBLISHERS   LITTLE ROCK

To Dear Old Maw, Mary Anne Brummett—
she knew I'd do something someday,
she just didn't know what—
and to Roy Hutchison, one damn good cowboy

Introduction

*T*he days of the trail drive to Ogallala are long since gone. "Teddy Blue" Abbott and Andy Adams and the other old boys have gone up the Long Trail years since. The days of the Wild West linger only on the silver screen—or in occasional gems like *Lonesome Dove*, which do their best to tell it like it really was.

But the cowboy isn't dead. That rascal is still hanging around the corral or the rodeo chute, swapping yarns, stretching the truth, and generally doing his best to live out the Good Old Days right now.

As Curt Brummett remembers growing up in eastern New Mexico, the Good Old Days were a little less than paradise. Being a one-time young sprout myself, who sprang up in urban El Paso (but "down the valley," where some of my friends had horses and we played serious cowboy), I appreciate Curt's early battles with reality.

When I was little, the Kids' Rodeo was special. We looked forward to it all year, told ourselves what wonders we would perform, and generally had to settle for being humiliated in the wild-cow milking contest. (Those old mothers had long since given up on lactating, but we had to run 'em down and give 'em a squeeze anyway.) A few of the boys and girls would compete like Real Cowboys and Cowgirls. The rest of us could only watch as they paraded in the grand entry and joined the blessed at each performance in the Kids' Rodeo arena.

Calf roping, barrel racing, and such were just dreams for most of us wanna-be cowboys and gals. Not so for Curt. He did it—and he still does it. Only a couple of years ago, I watched as he "headed" a steer so a world-famous cowboy could "heel" it—and the big name MISSED! I won't embarass the heeler by further identification, but I was plenty proud of Curt that day. If he'd had two ropes, I'll bet he could've headed *and* heeled that steer, but I reckon there have to be rules.

All this is by way of saying that Curt Brummett knows what he's writing about. He didn't watch from the grandstand while all the others covered themselves with dirt and glory; he done it hisself.

But when he starts telling stories about growing up, I'll admit I have reservations. Could any youngun have had *that* much fun in his trip "over Fools' Hill," as my mama used to call it? If you read Curt's stories or listen to him tell them in person, you'll swear it all happened exactly like he says—that he and Terry and Larry really did all those damfool things, really did incur the wrath and inspire the despair of parents and townfolk. Well, maybe. He says the Unholy Trio was held in such regard that the townspeople once "had complained to the authorities" because the Trio'd been standing around a suspiciously long time *without* causing any trouble. Made them nervous. Could it be he's telling the truth?

I feel for old Slimtech, Curt's teacher in the one-room schoolhouse. Even if he was 'leben feet tall, big around as a soda straw, and something of a pain in the... neck, no teacher should have had to put up with such shenanigans as he did. I can just see old Slimtech's mule, Lucifer, straightening out the curves in the trail thanks to a rigged lunch bucket or attack and pursuit by a mad stovepipe. Pore man didn't have a chance against the imagination of boys like Curt, who were devotedly and busily studying for the gallows. That fine old Western standard made famous in *Oklahoma!*, the auction of lunch baskets for a community fund-raising, is done to a turn, with old Slim-tech getting it in the end—well, no, I guess it was the boys got it *there*. At least they saved him from the dread manhunter, Widow Hausetter.

By the time Curt gets around to talking about Dear Old Dad and Dear Old Mom, you may wonder how they survived his growing up. Of course, unlike some modern Spock-trained parents, they did know what the bottom end of a child is for. What else do you do when a kid gets a rope, complete with instructions which he promptly disregards? "You didn't tell me not to do THAT," he says. It's true, though they'd figured anybody with one eye and half sense would know not to lasso a wild steer from the ground or parachute his sister out the barn loft or pull any number of other goofy (as Curt would call them) stunts this boy thought up.

His stories ring true. The one about "cowboy diaper rash" reminds me of one my mother told about a fellow who had the itch—that old-fashioned ailment that could drive a person crazy. She recommended he pat on a bit of Sloan's Liniment to soothe his feelings, but he—figuring that if a little is good, a lot is better—poured a whole bottle in the hot bath water. Folks around Canton, Mississippi, talked for years about what he looked like running down Main Street "in the altogether," as shy folks used to put it.

When you come right down to it, the mature Curt (if you'll pardon a bit of freedom with the language) ain't a lot smarter than the youngun. He reports ongoing idiocies much like those that characterized his earlier work with accomplices Larry and Terry. Makes you wonder if he needed accomplices. He does right well on his own as an adult, like when he hauls home in the Little Woman's sedan a pair of calves that are not car-trained, or encourages his grandson to spur a heretofore-tame quadruped into spectacular acrobatics while said grandson is on said quadruped's back. Maybe somebody ought to write a country-Western song called "Cowboys Don't Never Grow Up."

Reading Curt Brummett is like listening to him talk, standing there with his "slim, trim, athletic figure" (as he modestly describes it) pooched out over his belt buckle a couple of inches, towering over any podium folks can provide him. He writes like he talks, and he talks from the heart. He's been there. In fact, sometimes his language needs translating for folks who've never stepped in a steaming cow pie.

I don't know if he ever really had "a snake in the bathtub," as he claims in an earlier August House book by the same name, nor if he had as much trouble growing up as he says. (Did he and his pals sure enough store dynamite in the community outhouse? Sounds awfully like Vance Randolph's "Who Blowed Up the Church House?" but I reckon truth can be stranger than folklore sometimes.) Still, Curt Brummett will make you believe all he says is the gin-you-wine gospel truth. Or maybe the bottom line, instead, is, "If it ain't the way it was, it's the way it orta been."

John O. West
EL PASO, TEXAS

Contents

Life's Spice

*B*eing raised on a ranch swings between boring and exciting, and each to an extreme. There does not seem to be a way to find a happy medium. But then, one problem solves the other. You'd be surprised how things even out. Take the following example:

When the fall works was over, most of the older boys returned to school. Now, during that two months of solid labor, getting up at four in the morning and being on horseback fourteen or sixteen hours a day, you didn't have all that much time to create hate and discontent. You just didn't really feel like jiggerin' with anybody.

But after everyone finally settled down to the regular grind of school, boredom set in. Each day was the same as the last, and no matter how many mice you hid in a girl's desk or how much cayenne pepper you slipped into someone's lunch, nothing—and I mean nothing—livened things up for long.

So the area planning committee decided to have a box supper and dance. This kind of party was always a success. Everybody could get together, eat, dance, visit, and have a pretty good time, and the gossip that resulted from it would help put off the boredom for at least a week.

The single ladies always packed their suppers in a special way so there would be one or two of the single fellows to bid on their meal. The ladies figured they had bragging rights if their supper brought the highest bid.

The highest bidder on each boxed supper got the privilege of sharing it with the lady that fixed it. This pert near guaranteed a good meal with pleasant company.

In a ranching community, there are few secrets. This was especially true about the single people in our little area, mainly because all the older women would get together and compare gossip collected since the last local party.

The only tidbit of information at the time of the box supper that wasn't out-and-out gossip was that the school teacher, Mr. Ogleby Slimtech, and the area's resident manhunter, the widow Hausetter, were an item.

Now, Mr. Slimtech was as ugly as a mud fence, stood six-foot-five, and had feet the size of desk tops. He weighed in at about one hundred and fifty pounds of long, tall, and ugly. Until he started courting the widow Hausetter, he was a healthy one thirty-five. He was also prone to be very quiet except in the classroom.

This was a match made in heaven—Slimtech and the widow Hausetter. Of course, it was a match made by angels as bored as we'd been before the box supper.

The widow Hausetter was considered to be one of the best cooks in all of eastern New Mexico. Her biscuits would float right off a plate and melt in your mouth, and her pies were always the sweetest, lightest, and best-tasting. All that kept her single was the fact that she could talk the bark off a tree. Having been in her company a time or two myself, I can attest that this was not an exaggeration.

The widow had tried to trap every single man in the country at one time or another, but now she figured she had her one.

The three of us—Larry, Terry, and me—decided that if Slimtech was to get the manhunter's box supper, it was going to cost a bunch. We pooled our money and it totaled $8.45, which was a bunch. (Of course, the world-record box supper had brought $16.27 only two years before. It was made by the same widow, but never bought again by the same man. It seems the nonstop gab session just outweighed the perfect fried chicken and biscuits that defied gravity. After a decent meal and a couple of dances, the manhunter was hunting again.

Terry had been selected to bid for us because there were still a few people around town who thought he was a decent kid. We told him since people still kind of trusted him, he could probably pull it off. We *might* have mentioned that if he didn't do the bidding, we'd let it out that he was the one who sawed the floor boards through on the girl's outhouse. (We wouldn't have told on him, but he didn't know that. If you're gonna be a leader, you gotta do some harsh things.)

He like to've throwed a cat fit, but he agreed to bid.

The bidding started. Suppers went from two dollars to four-and-a-half, and the community fund was thriving. When the auctioneer got to the widow Hausetter's basket of good grub, there was several bachelors there waiting. They knew what kind of eating pleasure was in store if they could just get that basket bought.

"Two dollars," came a holler from the back of the room. It belonged to a sure-nuff hungry cowboy from the Cross L's.

The auctioneer casually mentioned that two dollars wasn't near enough, 'cause he just bid three-seventy-five.

Slimtech finally got in on the act. He very calmly bid ten dollars, which he said he reckoned ought to just about buy that basket of groceries. He had a mean-looking snarl on his face when he said it.

He was right.

His bid proved that true love could not be obstructed by financial double-dealing and that he knew about our plot to up the ante. The latter was clear because as he bid with one hand, he had the other covering Terry's mouth.

There was going to be some more dancing and visiting before everyone settled down to serious eating.

Larry, Terry, and me got back together. While we were talking about Slimtech out-bidding us, and smirking a little about how he could've bought that supper for eight-fifty, we got this other idea.

And just barely in time. Several of the adults had seen us three standing there minding our own business and had complained to the authorities.

So my dad and Larry's dad came over and told us to split up. People were getting nervous because we had been talking together for close on to half an hour and nothing had happened yet. Terry's mom figured a little preventive maintenance was in order. Boy, if you ever get caught messing up just *one time*, they don't ever forget it.

But, not to worry. Our plan was fixing to go into action.

Terry and me would create a little bit of distraction, and Larry would execute the main course. Literally.

Us distractors chose a couple of young ladies and asked them to dance. From there, things went right on downhill.

I got the best looking of the two, and that ain't saying much. Being raised on a ranch, you learn to live with minor setbacks, and the old gal I had chose to dance with was about as minor as they come. But we had made our plans, and now we had to stay with 'em.

Terry'd forgotten the plan. Shoot, Terry had forgotten who he was. He was moon-eyed and actually being nice to the silly thing he was dancing with. That left it all up to me.

I noticed Larry was in position, so I created a small distraction. I casually mentioned to the lady I was dancing with that even though one eye was a different color from the other and her feet weren't much bigger than a table top, she seemed to be able to dance fairly good.

Now let me say this: I've been hit pretty hard by a couple of men and I've been kicked by one or two horses, but I have *never* been whopped as hard by anything as by that old gal.

When I quit sliding across the dance floor and finally shook the flashing lights out of my eyes, I noticed there was a lynch mob forming up. And my Dear Old Dad was leading 'em.

It took quite a while to convince everyone that I was just joking and to make my apologies to the lady. (Some lady.)

They said I could stay, but I had to keep my mouth shut and leave that poor defenseless girl alone. I agreed to the terms—quickly, I might add.

While everyone was talking about hanging me, Larry was doing his part. He made it to the manhunter's basket and added just a touch more salt (actually a lot more salt) to the gravy, potato salad, and lemon pie, but not before stashing a chicken leg in his coat pocket.

Everything settled down nicely. People were quietly enjoying their meals when there came a muffled roar.

Slimtech made a dash for the punch bowl holding his mouth. He tripped, fell face first into Giles Jakemon's chocolate pie, and knocked off a pot of chile into Annie Fykicker's lap. Goodbye, boredom.

Slimtech finally got the pie off his face and enough water down him to wash out the salt, and they all got to comparing notes. That was after Annie got her clothes back on.

I'm not sure how the Christians felt just before they were thrown out to them big cats, but if I thought about it a while, I could probably give you a fair rendition. Faith is okay, but I believe there is a limit to its endurance.

Here come the crowd.

Slimtech had never talked so much or so fast since he had lived here. The manhunter was speechless and weepy because someone had ruined her supper. Larry, Terry, and me was getting nervous. Me and Terry had an alibi—I had a caved-in head to prove it.

Everyone was staring at Larry, who had his hands in his coat pockets. Asked if he knew anything about the old salt-in-the-supper trick, he pulled his hands out and shrugged. When he did, he also pulled out a chicken leg that had snagged on his cuff. (Greed is a terrible thing.)

That was when I got to thinking about them Christians and big cats.

After a council meeting, it was declared that I had created the distraction while Larry did the damage, and Terry was guilty by association. It was also decided that the punishment should fit the crime. Since we fixed the supper, they said, we would eat it.

Maybe them lions wouldn't of been all that bad after all.

Everyone but us had a good laugh while we ate that seasoned-up food. They only thing good about it was Larry hadn't salted the chicken, and neither did we.

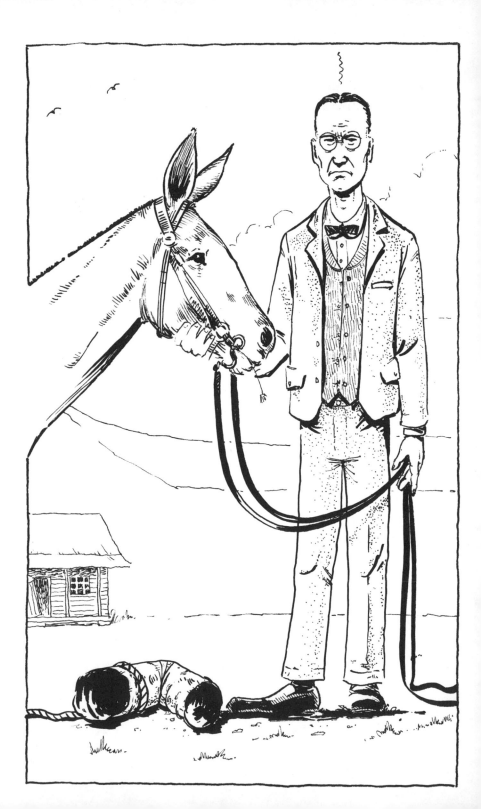

The Attack of the Stovepipe

Going to school in eastern New Mexico can be about as dangerous as pregnancy-testing mountain lions in their natural habitat. And there was a time or two when getting home from school was a triumph of survival.

My brothers and I rode horses to school, about nine miles each way. There were several times that nine-mile trip was a way yonder more exciting than most people would care to think about, much less live through.

From the time we left our place until we got to the school, our little makeshift cavalry would grow in numbers. Some kids would be riding burros, others horses, and there might even be a mule or two. I've always wondered what such a ragtag bunch must have looked like coming out of the hills and swarming down on the schoolhouse. I bet it was quite a comical sight.

Going to school was not the most fun part of our lives. Though we tolerated it, we didn't really enjoy it. Adding to the unenjoyable part was the fact that three miles from school we had to pick up our teacher, Mr. Ogleby Slimtech.

The older boys made a little extra money by breaking horses for other ranches. What better way is there to break a horse than to ride him eighteen miles a day and expose him to all forms of civilization, or something like it? Besides, riding broncs can produce unexpected entertainment.

Old Slimtech rode an eight-year-old mule he had bought from our dad. This mule was as goofy as a drunk chicken and not near as reliable. The old man had told Slimtech the mule wasn't to be trusted, but the teacher wanted that mule and so he bought him. The teacher and the mule got along pretty good until there were one or two unplanned events.

It didn't take long. It was only about the fourth or fifth day before the last three miles to school got pretty exciting.

All of us kids came down the trail, and you could hear lunch pails rattling against saddles and us talking and laughing. Then Old Slimtech would ride out from his house on Lucifer, and all the joy would come to a halt. We noticed, too, that Slimtech's lunch bucket never rattled after the fourth or fifth time he rode Lucifer to school. It seemed Lucifer didn't appreciate being used as a pack mule to haul noisy lunch buckets.

What had happened was, Old Slimtech had tied his lunch bucket to the saddle, mounted Lucifer, and the mule went tee-totally crazy. As soon as Lucifer noticed a strange clanking sound coming from his left shoulder, he sold out. He swallowed his head, jumped high and hard to the right, and at the same time tried to kick that lunch bucket plumb out of the county. Not being able to get this done, he pulled a one-mule stampede. He might not have gone quite so crazy if Old Slimtech hadn't screamed like a gut-shot panther.

My brother, realizing Slimtech wasn't any part of a horseman *or* muleteer, spurred his bronc and tried to catch old Lucifer and our helpless schoolteacher. The last thing we saw as they dropped out of sight down a shallow canyon was a runaway mule, a terrified schoolteacher, and my older brother fixing to rope one or the other of 'em.

Though he didn't want to admit it, Old Slimtech was tickled pink that the seventh loop caught Lucifer. He couldn't decide whether Joe missed those first six loops on purpose or not. Joe was considered to be a pretty good roper, and Old Slimtech kind of suspected he might have missed those loops just so's he could chase 'em all over those hills.

School got started about three hours later than usual that day.

One day just before Christmas vacation, there was a special feeling in the morning air. Each kid in our little cavalry, from the youngest to the oldest, was in the holiday spirit, making jokes and laughing at each other. When Old Slimtech joined us that day, we all stayed in a good mood. He was even acting like *he* was maybe having a good time.

Before he got to school that morning, though, he would want to kill each one of us. Well, maybe not the younger ones, because they could still be taught left from right, but anyone over the age of seven, he'd have liked to throttle.

Tom and Joe were riding broncs and having quite a time showing off for the rest of us. They would break free from the group and race to a jack pine and then stampede back to the group screaming like charging Apaches, all to the delight of us younger kids. Especially me. I idolized those two for their ability to ride and rope. I longed for the day when I could ride green-broke mountain horses to school instead of the more settled ranch horses.

Little did I know that my settled old ranch horse was going to be the one to cause yet another setback in the educational progress of our great nation. See, between Slimtech's place and the schoolhouse there was an old abandoned cabin with a stovepipe. The wall of the cabin wasn't but two or three feet from the edge of the road. What happened was the horse's fault. If he hadn't of gone so close to that old abandoned cabin, I wouldn't of ever roped that stovepipe.

As the group came closer to the cabin, Old Slimtech made the older boys calm down and ride beside him at the head of the group. He said they were scaring the other children with their wild and reckless actions. Actually, old Lucifer was acting like he wanted to join the fun, and Slimtech wasn't up to being chased all over the country again by some seventeen-year-old maniac swinging a rope. The boys calmed down and rode in beside old killjoy.

While Tom and Joe and them were showing off and being called down, I was playing with my catch rope. I had been wanting to show off just a little myself, but since there wasn't any maverick bulls or wild black stallions to capture, I figured the best I could to was to rope the stovepipe on that old cabin.

As soon as I threw the loop, I had a feeling that I had done messed up. Talk about a right feeling. Right then, I started trying to figure out how I was going to get my rope back. Boy, was I silly. I found out in the next three or four seconds that getting the rope back was going to be a way yonder easier than straightening out all them other little problems that had developed.

Before I could get my horse stopped and ask for help, the sound of my whaleline scraping on that rusty pipe had already spooked him. The rope tightened, making the pipe really squeak. Now, all that noise plus a tight rope attracted attention. My horse, having had a previous opportunity to observe Lucifer, pulled a one-critter stampede. Everyone saw it but Slimtech and Lucifer. They didn't need to, 'cause in about two seconds they was gonna be right in the middle of it.

I sure never thought that old horse could pull down a whole building. He could, though. And when boards started breaking, horses started leaving. Yep, there was kids screaming, burros braying, and dogs barking in the road.

When we finally got to the end of any moving parts, that old horse kept trying to go. He was trying to buck and run away all at the same time. Each time he hit the end of the rope, it kind of stalled him out. After about twice of that, the stovepipe come loose. Passed us like a bullet. By now, any critter that could run was doing so, and my old horse, not wanting to be left alone with a renegade stovepipe on the loose, figured he better catch up with some of the others. Since him and old Lucifer had run together in the same pastures, he just naturally figured they should run down the road together. And he proceeded to catch up.

It is hard to run from something that is tied to you. It is, I might add, pert near impossible to escape it. But as we caught up to Lucifer and Slimtech, that old stovepipe took a bounce for the worse. Lucifer figured my horse was the one the stovepipe was after, so he slowed down just a hair. At this same time, the stovepipe came off my rope and bounced right into Lucifer's rear end. Old Lucifer gained some country.

Seems one of the guy wires on the stovepipe snagged in the mule's tail. As Slimtech and Lucifer passed through town and crossed the river, some people heard him holler something about justifiable homicide in between his terror-filled screams for help.

It only took an hour or two to regroup and gather all the kids and horses and burros and mules. Tom had been bucked off right at the start of this mess and Joe's horse had took off towards the river, but they were back and laughing. I knew they weren't gonna kill me, but I still had to face Old Slimtech.

About three that afternoon, Old Slimtech and Lucifer came to school. Both of 'em looked like someone had poured a sack full of bobcats on 'em.

Slimtech was so glad to be alive, he wasn't even gonna punish me. Yet. Said the way he figured it, if it hadn't been for those two cowboys running him down, he'd have been in Fort Sumner by dark.

He dismissed what was left of the class, and we headed home. Everyone was riding just like always, except Old Slimtech.

When I asked him why he was walking and leading old Lucifer, he glared at me. And when I tried to show him how sorry I really was by offering to let him ride double with me, he just kind of went blank. That's when I rode off and left him and Lucifer, him talking about some kind of conspiracy and Lucifer agreeing with him.

THREE

Ruled by the Clock

*I*t was spring, and school was just about over for the
year. It would be out for us three weeks earlier than for
the rest of the kids because of the spring cattle works. I
sure was glad to hear the old man say I could go with them
this time. Usually I had to wait until school was out and
then catch up. Spring cow works meant six to ten weeks
of roundups, branding, roping, and pretty good times, all
of which comes in the form of long hard hours a-horseback,
flanking calves, and smelling dust and burnt hair.

My older brothers decided that since it was my first
time to make the whole works, we needed to leave school
in a flash of glory. We had to pull something special. We
discussed burning down the schoolhouse, but that did
seem a mite drastic. We discussed kidnapping Old Slimtech, but we didn't want to do anything that would get
anybody hurt—or us caught.

As we were riding to school one morning and Slimtech came to meet us, I got a pretty good idea.

You may recall that Old Slimtech's mule, Lucifer, had
a tendency to blow up, stampede, or go just plumb crazy
for the least of reasons, such as lunch pails rattling or
stovepipes attacking him.

The nice thing about this mule blowing smooth up was that it was always about three hours before he could be calmed down and things could even start to get back to normal.

Old Lucifer was going to help us out.

I was so proud of my idea that I didn't even want to share it with anybody. I decided I would just pull it off myself. Besides, I had a score to settle with our local educator. Old Slimtech thought everything that had happened to him that year was my fault. And he did have a good memory. Every time we started to eat lunch, he very carefully tested his to make sure it hadn't been jiggered with. And riding to and from school, him and old Lucifer had taken to riding at the back of the bunch where he could keep an eye out for someone silly enough to try and pull a joke on him or on old Lucifer. He justified me cutting firewood every day for the school stove by saying, "You're not just building your body, you're building your mind," but everyone else just figured as long as he could hear that axe splitting wood, he knew where I was.

Yep, I was gonna enjoy leaving school early.

The time was getting close, and I was so tickled I could hardly stand it.

Old Slimtech kept an alarm clock on his desk so's he could make sure each lesson on each subject had equal time. He would set the alarm for a certain length of time, and when it went off, it meant that one subject was finished for the day. Slimtech had a precise schedule, and when it was complete, school was over for the day. He would close his books, place them on the shelf, put his lunch pail by the alarm clock on the desk, and then go outside to saddle Lucifer. After making sure everything was put up and everyone had already left or was fixing to, he would pick up his lunch pail, lock up the building, tie the pail to old Lucifer, lead him fifteen or twenty feet to make sure he wasn't going to do anything harsh, and then mount up.

Well, the last day of school was upon us, and I was some excited. I had my plan all timed. Actually, it was quite simple.

Since it was my last day, I volunteered to cut an extra batch of firewood about fifteen minutes before school was out. This caused Slimtech to spill a bottle of ink and go into a minor smothering spell, but he accepted my offer. Just because he was a schoolteacher didn't mean he wasn't dumb.

My timing was perfect. I was bringing in a load of firewood just as Slimtech was going out to saddle old Lucifer. I chunked the wood into the woodbox, grabbed the alarm clock, set it for what I thought was five minutes, and packed it inside the lunch pail. I was leaving to get my horse as Slimtech was coming back. He even commented on the fact that someday I might amount to something.

I mentioned he had better hurry, or he was gonna have to ride home by hisself. He knew we were in an excited state because of the cow works, so he just grabbed his lunch pail and followed me out. Tom and Joe had my horse saddled and ready. They were grinning something fierce.

Tom said our farewell party was about to begin.

Seems they had cut the saddle strings on one side of the cantle so when Lucifer started trotting, the slicker would slip to one side and cause a mild stampede.

I just laughed and said that wasn't nothing. I told 'em to watch as Slimtech led Lucifer out. I figured that clock ought to go off about the time he was ready to turn around and get mounted. Something I failed to mention: until that day I had never even touched an alarm clock.

Old Slimtech got on Lucifer, and we started for home. We had made about a quarter of a mile and nothing had happened. Not even the slicker had slipped. I was getting depressed. We had completely given up and was about to forget the whole thing when everything blowed up at once.

The alarm clock finally went off, and Lucifer held true to form. He side-jumped and kicked. By now, though, Slimtech had that move down pat, and he weathered the first part of the storm pretty easy. But Lucifer wasn't done with it. He'd made up his mind the lunch pail had to go, and he started bucking like none of us had ever seen. The only reason Slimtech was staying on was because that crazy mule kept bucking back in under him.

Tom decided he better ride in and pick up that goofy old mule, and right then the slicker came loose. The slicker hit Tom's horse right between the eyes and caused him to get pretty silly, too. While I was laughing at Tom, Lucifer and Old Slimtech passed us in an all-out one-mule stampede. All you could hear was a muffled alarm clock bell, a braying mule, and Old Slimtech screaming something about revenge.

I believe his exact words were, "If I live through this, I'll guarantee that you three won't."

With those immortal words drifting through the clear eastern New Mexico air, him and old Lucifer went out of sight into a shallow canyon.

Three or four days later, a couple of cowboys rode into camp about suppertime. They were pretty well up on news of the local area, and they were free with all of their information. One little tidbit of news that gave me a chance to breathe easier was the story of how the school-teacher finally made it to school one morning kind of late.

They said he looked terrible and was mumbling something about lynch mobs and vigilantes, outlaw kids, and goofy mules.

Seems as though when old Lucifer finally quit running and Slimtech got off, he just unsaddled the mule and turned him loose, and he started walking back to town. After he had calmed down enough to where he could make any sense, he just quit talking. That's a fact. He just quit.

He walked home and turned in his resignation.

Rumor has it that he hired out as a piano player in a house of joy somewhere down by the border where there weren't any mules or alarm clocks, and no kids were allowed around at any time.

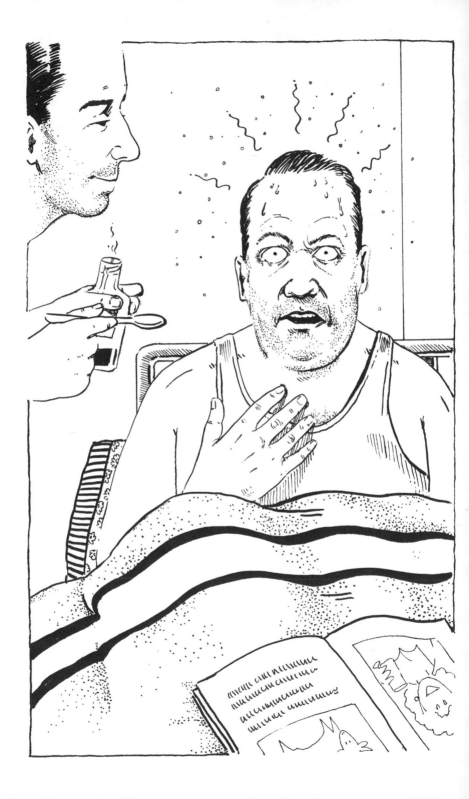

FOUR

Range Country Remedies

When I decided at a very early age to be a cowboy, I wasn't aware of some of the occupational draw-backs. Oh, I knew about the long hours, the miserable working conditions, and the fact that you could make more money selling pop bottles. But I had been raised to accept things not going just the way they should, so I wasn't too upset about those job hazards.

What really did bother me was the fact that everyone over the age of twenty-five figured they was some kind of general practical doctor. After my first experience with sickness at a cow camp, I promised myself should I ever get sick, I would not tell anyone but the first real doctor I could get to. And if you want to know, every time I've broken that promise, I've deeply regretted it.

I was just out of high school and had hired out to a ranch up in the Torrington, Wyoming, country.

When I got there, quite a bit of snow was on the ground and a bunch more falling. I had left New Mexico because we were having a pretty bad winter, and I didn't have enough sense to realize the farther north you went, the worse the weather got. But I had hired out, and I figured I would stay awhile. It was the most cold and snow I had ever been in.

The ranch had two camps for married men and a big bunkhouse at the headquarters for single men. I liked everybody in the bunkhouse, but the help did keep changing. Most of the work was feeding (and very little cowboying), and with all that snow on the ground, feeding was not fun.

After I had been there for about two weeks, the foreman, name of Bob, hired an old boy from Florida. Cleotis was a drifter, and you could tell he hadn't ever done any hard work. He was fat and lazy and smelled like a wet coyote. All he could do was gripe about the weather and the equipment. The only thing he liked was the food. Still, we needed some help on the feed wagons, and help was getting hard to find.

After about two weeks of working in the snow and getting a little wet, he caught a cold, and the poor old fat thing really got to complaining.

Now, I had been around some sick people a time or two, but I had never seen anyone that coughed as much or was as helpless as Cleotis. He would just lay around and cough and complain. He coughed so much at night, we couldn't get any sleep.

The foreman offered to take him to the doctor, but the old fat thing was afraid the doctor might cure him and he would have to go back to work. All the rest of us was wishing he would either get well or die.

During the worst part of the sick man's spell, I managed to get a day off and go to town. Among my purchases was a couple of cans of jalapeños. I had a craving for some spicy food, and I fully intended to flavor up breakfast the next morning.

When I got back to the ranch that evening, Bob had had about all the coughing he could stand. Fact is, he was a hair short of ready to put the old chronic out of his misery. I believe the other hands would have sworn to the fact that the lazy thing had just committed suicide.

As I was putting up my new shirt and levis, Bob noticed my canned peppers. He came over and offered me two dollars for one can. I may be a little goofy every now and then, but when I see a chance for a profit, I take it. He paid me, took the peppers, and went to his little room at the end of the bunkhouse.

After a while, he came out and visited with a couple of the other hands kind of quiet-like. I noticed that every now and then, one would sneak a peek at Cleotis and nod his head. Well, after a five-minute summit, old Bob walked over to the stricken man holding a medicine bottle with some terrible-looking green stuff in it.

He told Cleotis he had just found some cough syrup he'd forgotten he had, and he thought it would do some good if he took some right away. Cleotis assured Bob he didn't really need any medicine, because he felt like the cold was just about over. Bob and the other hands suggested that if he didn't take at least two spoons of the syrup on his own, they would give him the whole bottle with a drench gun. He had his choice, but any way it went, they figured on getting some sleep.

Well, he took the first big spoonful of that green mess and pert near had a smothering spell. Before he could get his breath, Bob and another hand had forced the second spoonful down his throat.

I've seen critters fight their heads before, but never had I seen some of what this poor old thing pulled. Cleotis went off the end. He grabbed his throat, fell over backwards, rolled on the floor croaking, and crawled for the water bucket.

A couple of the hands was worrying they might've killed him, a couple was wishing they had, and I was holed up at the head of my bunk hoping he wouldn't try to kill us all if he lived through it, whatever it was.

When the poor old thing finally got his breath, he wanted to know just what the hell kind of medicine he had been forced to take and why his throat was burning like a runaway volcano.

Bob told him it was just about the best cough syrup money could buy. It contained plenty of jalapeño peppers so as to burn out any infection in his throat and belly, and the other sixty percent was mineral oil. Everyone knew what the mineral oil was for: it was to help the jalapeños slip right on through his system after they finished killing all those little germs that kept him coughing all the time.

You know, that cough syrup went to work almost immediately. Seems like after he found out what was in it, he didn't much want to cough. I guess he didn't want to strain any unnecessary muscles. He didn't sleep much that night, mainly because he spent most of it in the outhouse, but the rest of us got a pretty good night's sleep, though every now and then someone would wake up laughing.

Since then, I have seen a number of different cures, some applied with the best of intentions and some with puredee murder in mind.

Like the time we was branding a bunch of late calves on a place just north of Texico. We had a pretty good crew and was getting along just fine in spite of the fact that the boss's nephew was helping us.

He was nineteen and thought he knew just about everything that was needed to be known about everything—everything, that is, except how to flank calves or otherwise work around livestock. He had been raised in Yankeeville, USA, and although it wasn't a proven fact, we suspected he might have been weaned a little late and then raised up on hot cereals and puddings. Truth is, it wasn't just the fact that he didn't know how to work that made us dislike him. It was the fact that he was *there*.

Somehow or other I got stuck with him on the flanking. After about eight or nine head of them big calves eating me alive because he wouldn't do his share of holding, I began to get mad. Well, I had learned several years before not to get too mad, just to go on and get even. I started plotting against the darling little know-it-all.

A couple of the hands told me to let him have the head and me take the heels. At least that way, I could know I wasn't going to get kicked. Well, that made sense. After a couple of calves, I figured he needed to know how to flank one if the roper decided to bring it to us by the neck.

I asked the roper to neck a couple so I could show our little Yankee how to do it. Now, them calves was black Bramer cross and big, but I got the first three on the ground and managed to make it look easy. I just waited till one tried to jump and kick, and then I just went with him and put him on the ground. I told the kid to stay back till I got one on the ground, 'cause he was probably too weak to be much help on a deal like that.

He took the bait. Ego is a terrible thing.

The roper figured out right quick what I had just done and, him being the helpful type, helped me out. He necked a calf that weighed about three hundred and fifty pounds and headed for the fire. I stepped back and said, "Here you go, Junior, show your stuff."

I think it was this calf made Junior decide to become a politician.

It was a terrible sight. That calf was jumping as high as the rope would let him, and he reached about twenty feet to kick a cowboy that was just trying to get out of the way.

Junior waded into him. That calf took off Junior's cap and Steelers T-shirt the first jump, and on the way down from his second jump, he put a hind foot in Junior's right front pants pocket. Now, Junior might've been quick to mouth off, but he wasn't a complete dummy. He realized right away that there wasn't enough room in those pants for him and the calf both, and he decided to give them up. The calf agreed with Junior and took them.

All Junior got out of this little experience was a gap in his wardrobe and a lot of skinned places. There was signs that he had been in the wrong place at the wrong time. His legs looked like someone had taken a shoeing rasp and tried to trim 'em down. It wasn't anything serious, but he needed a little medical attention, you know, just to get cleaned up, and some disinfectant put on to prevent gangrene.

What happened next is hard to describe.

Two of the hands each got a can of pinkeye spray, and then with a nod of the head, made a pass down one leg apiece. I have never seen anyone move that quick before.

Yep, he moved smooth over his uncle just as he was coming through the gate to see why we were shut down. He flew over two fences and one hundred and seventy-five cows to get to the water tank. He probably won't ever be a diving champion, but he can get in the water all right.

His uncle was pretty opened-minded about the whole thing. He even grinned a little when we explained what had happened. He took Junior back to the house, and we finished branding. I have often wondered if Junior ever let anybody doctor on him after that.

I've had some first-hand experience with impromptu medical treatment like that, too—and I don't like it. Even when they mean well, they can still get you hurt or make you hurt yourself.

One, and only one, time, I traded for a saddle with a padded seat. I had ridden this saddle a time or two at a couple of ropings, and I just had to have it. Well, I liked this saddle and started using it just about all the time, instead of just for roping. That was my first mistake. The second was not giving that padded seat time to dry after it had been rained on for about three weeks early one fall.

Some of you may have guessed the type of ailment that I developed, but for those that have never been in a similar situation, I'll explain. I kind of got a little gallded. Actually, not a little—all the way around from one knee to the other. Sort of a cowboy diaper rash.

No matter what I tried, I couldn't clear it up. I had been married about a year, and the Little Woman couldn't figure out how to help me. Of course, I didn't just tell everybody about my tender situation. It seemed about the time the rash started clearing up, it would come another rain and I would start all over again. People think they get grouchy when they try to quit smoking—they ain't seen grouchy.

The Little Woman and me had been invited to a party that was to have plenty of food, drink, and dancing. We both liked to dance and we figured on going, but the day of the party, things got worse. I mean big-time worse. I had spent all day sorting steers and getting things straightened out in a couple of pastures that had gotten mixed. It had been hot and muggy all day and me riding a damp saddle and sweating like crazy. My lower area was on fire. I was hurting so bad, I would've cried if I thought it would help. When I finally got to the house that evening, I was not in any mood to go dancing. I couldn't hardly walk, much less dance.

I finally got the Little Woman calmed down and told her if she could find something to ease the pain, we'd go. I will never make such a deal again.

She wanted to go to that dance pretty bad—so bad, in fact, she caused me to pull a one-man stampede and pert near drown myself trying to undo what she had just had me do to myself.

She went through the medicine cabinet looking for anything that might even come close to easing my pain. She found some kind of lotion that had *Cali*-something on it, and the directions said to "apply liberally to affected area." She read on just to be sure. This bottle of lotion was showing signs of being very old and we had no idea where, when, or why we'd gotten it. She read it was good for insect bites and stings. Then there was a faded place and the word "rash."

I told her I would try it. Talk about loose lips.

I went to the bathroom, took off my clothes, and applied liberally to the affected area. I guess I made a lot more noise that I normally do when I take a shower, 'cause when the Little Woman finally got the door open and came inside to see why I was cussing, the unfeeling old bat fell down on the floor laughing.

I might have looked a little ridiculous—mainly because the affected area was burning like Hades itself. It was so hot, I couldn't figure out why it wasn't smoking. And I'll tell you something else: it's tough to chew somebody out when you're standing on your head in a shower with cold water running down your chest and into your face. It's also pretty hard to take someone's apology serious when they can't hardly talk for laughing.

After the fire got down to a slow smolder, I got up the nerve to get dressed. By the time we got to the party, the little woman had just about quit laughing and the affected area was numb.

We never did figure out what that lotion was for, and we haven't seen any of it in any stores, but I got rid of that bottle. And anytime I get to feeling poorly or get hurt, I make dern sure I'm the only one that knows about it.

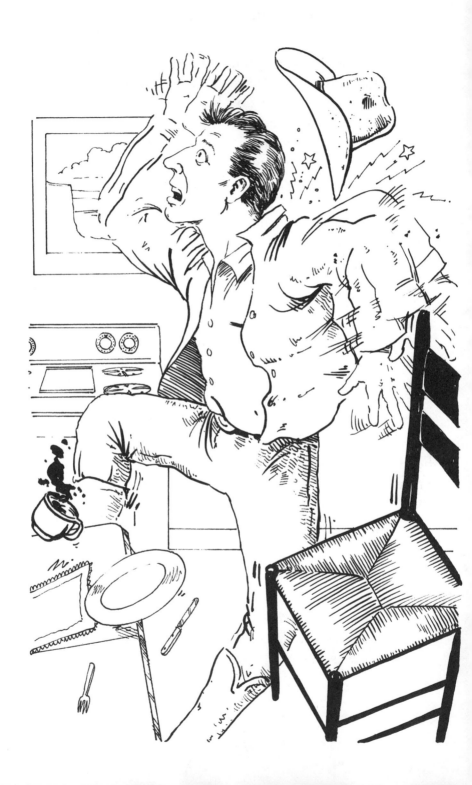

FIVE

Stinging Things

Contrary to what you might guess, springtime in the sand hills isn't all that much fun. Just because things are greening up and the calves are slick, fat, and sassy doesn't mean everything's hunky-dory.

Now, don't get me wrong. I enjoy seeing everything green up and the new calves start growing, but I'm not crazy about a few of the other things nice warm weather brings out. I mean scorpions and yellowjackets. I have had some exciting experiences with these and like critters. The uproar caused by the irritable little varmints can be compared to a police raid on a little old ladies' bingo parlor—it ain't that big a deal, but no one really wants any part of it.

It had been raining and misting for about three days in a row one spring, and it was just a touch cooler than normal. I guess the weather had made a few of the wilder critters hunt some form of protection from the elements.

As I was getting ready to leave one cool, damp morning, the Little Woman suggested I take a jacket, preferably the one I had hung up on the floor by the kitchen door. I commented that should I decide to take a jacket, I would take whichever one I wanted. I said this kind of under my breath as I picked up the jacket and began to put it on. I mean—you know how it is—there wasn't any point in stirring up the Little Woman over something as silly as a jacket.

About the time I started buttoning up, I noticed a slight discomfort along my left arm. It felt like someone was trying to put out about twenty-seven ceegars all in the same spot. I managed to get the jacket off with some difficulty. I found you can take a lined Levi jacket off in thirty or forty quick, precise moves and still keep the damage to the surrounding area at a minimum. I didn't, but you can.

By the time I had danced around, knocked the coffee pot off the table, run smooth over the Little Woman, and got shed of the jacket, I had things in a bit of a mess.

Meanwhile, Jughead (our pitbull-Queensland heeler crossbred cowdog pup) took it on hisself to protect the Little Woman—and took after me. It's bad enough to try putting out a range fire on your arm, helping the Little Woman up, and fighting off an overly protective mutt, but when the one you're helping causes the one you're fighting to fight more, it can get plumb out of hand.

I finally let the Little Woman fall back to the floor, grabbed that idiot dog, and threw him out the back door. Then I checked on my arm.

As I took off what was left of my shirt, the Little Woman picked up what was left of my jacket and shook out three scorpions. They were big enough to replace one of them horses that pulls that refreshment wagon at state fairs and parades. Fact is, I don't see how I managed to pick *up* that jacket with them three inside it.

My arm was hurting and swelling fast. Jughead was still standing at the kitchen door growling like a big dog, and the Little Woman was in the process of killing the last of the stinging horses.

I'm the type of person that's allergic to ant bites, bee stings, and extremely harsh criticism. I had pills for the first two, but I usually have to find an understanding neighbor to help with the last one. The way my arm was hurting, I figured I could put up with the uncouth comments from the Little Woman concerning the spilt coffee.

As the Little Woman gave me my pills, she actually showed some concern—even if it wasn't but for three or four seconds. She mentioned that I had better go to the doctor and see if I needed any other kind of medicine.

I agreed. Those pills seemed to help but I was feeling kind of flighty. I went to start the car while the Little Woman was changing out of her coffee-stained clothes. She always did pick some strange times to look stylish. She came out about the time I finally got the car started and pulled up to the front door.

She had brought me another shirt and made me change while the car was warming up. My arm is swelling up and fixing to bust plumb off, and she's worried about my general appearance.

The Little Woman decided since we were going to town anyway, we should take Jughead with us and get his rabies shot. I think she was being cute.

So Jughead got in the back seat, and the Little Woman started driving. It's only about thirty miles to town, but with the Little Woman chewing me out about the coffee and knocking her down, it didn't seem to be more than about eighty or so.

As the doctor was shooting me, I tried to explain the teeth marks on my hand. The sight of a needle makes me a little nervous, though, so I figured I'd just let the Little Woman handle it. She did.

She said, "Oh, he just gets too excited over nothing, and when he does, so does my puppy."

Puppy, my foot. The sucker weighs forty pounds and is still growing.

The doctor (who used to be a friend) mentioned we might get Jughead a rabies shot, considering what all he had been chewing on in the last couple of days.

The shot I got from the doctor didn't do much for the swelling, but it sure made me feel better, so I suggested that the Little Woman do some grocery shopping while I took the pup to the vet.

After I let the Little Woman out at the local Safeway, it seemed to me the heater was working a little too good in that old car. I went to turn it off, and that's when I got my first clue that things weren't just what they should be. The heater wasn't on. It had been, but it wasn't now.

About two blocks from the grocery store, Jughead started snapping and growling. Of course, the first thing I thought of was *RABIES*. The next thing I thought of was giving him the car.

I turned around to see just exactly what the problem was and got stung right between the eyes by a kamikaze yellowjacket. I guess that nice warm air and them smooth New Mexico roads had kind of upset the little critters.

For the moment, I forgot about driving and started swatting yellowjackets, while trying to find the door latch. Yep, there was a whole herd of them stinging critters, and it appeared that all of 'em was upset.

Some days it just don't pay to get up.

It was about the same time I noticed the second or eighth sting that I also noticed the car jump a curb.

Somehow I missed the thirty-one cars in the immediate vicinity—each carrying two to four witnesses—and made it through the stoplight. (Now, this town isn't all that big, and you would think that by 9:30 in the morning, everyone would either be at work, school, or anywhere besides where I was.)

The damage wasn't all that bad. I got the sign advertising three burritos for ninety-nine cents with the purchase of one gallon of Paula Sue's Special Soda Pop. Course the sign was posted on the door of Paula Sue's new Lincoln towncar.

After the yellowjackets, the police, and the insurance people left and I got Jughead calmed down, I called my friend Mike to go pick up the Little Woman and bring her to the scene of the wreck.

I had only been stung three or four times, but I sure did hurt. My eyes were almost swelled shut, and I didn't want to take a chance on getting into a car wreck.

By the time Mike and the Little Woman got there, I was sicker than a poisoned pup. And Jughead had a few whelps on his head. This had not been a good day.

Mike took the pup to the vet and said he would meet us at the doctor's office. We headed to the shot shop.

Two shots and a thirty-minute lecture on never slapping at a bee or yellowjacket later, the doctor said I could go home. He also suggested I stay in bed for a day or two and give the swelling time to go down.

To say I was getting paranoid about things touching me would be an understatement. I pert near bailed out of the car a half dozen times because I thought something was crawling on me. I was sure nuff spooky.

As I was laying around the house waiting for the swelling to go down, we decided to go to Clovis to the horse sale the next day.

When we went to bed, I noticed the Little Woman's head was considerable larger than usual. She had a pickup load of curlers in her hair and some kind of bed sheet or tarp holding 'em in place. No big deal. If she wanted to put herself through that kind of torture just to look good, it was okay with me.

Sometime around 2:30 that morning, I felt something stinging the small of my back.

I pulled a one-man stampede.

Everywhere I went, whatever it was followed me. I couldn't seem to get rid of the covers, and every time I went up, the critter was under me when I came down. I was slapping the bed, hollering about a fourteen-pound scorpion with six of his kinfolks helping out.

This upset the Little Woman just a tad. She's not that easy to get along with when she wakes up on her own, and this sudden commotion wasn't helping her disposition any.

What with me making all that racket, her goofy pup came into the bedroom to get in on the act. He did very well for just a puppy.

Since it was dark, he just bit anything that was handy. I don't think the Little Woman would've gotten in such a hurry if he hadn't bit her. Something seemed to inspire her to quicker action.

By the time the Little Woman got a light on, the dog locked in the hall, and me off the top of the dresser, she pulled the covers off the bed. And right there in the middle of it, lying in wait for their next victim, was two of the most vicious-looking hair curlers I have ever seen.

I blew smooth up.

Very few times have I ever laid the law down, but that night about nine years ago, I laid down a law that hasn't been broken yet. I made it pretty clear.

Should the need arise for the Little Woman to sleep with them spiny little things in her hair, she will do so in the pickup, the barn, or the pasture. And she will take that goofy pup with her.

For pert near nine years now, when I go to bed each night, I reach over and pat the Little Woman on the head. That's just to make sure that if I roll over on something that stings I have a plenty good reason to pull a one-man stampede.

SIX

Grandmas Are
a Fearsome Lot

*A*bout this time every year, I get to thinking about all
the past events of the summer, you know, ropings
and things like that. But this fall, I'm a little worried about
other things: mainly, I'm concerned about the Little
Woman.

The fact of the matter is I've decided to think about
that age-old subject of many thinkers. Yep, I'm going to
ponder on grandmothers and mothers. In this particular
instance, both are the same.

Now, I've been married to the same mother-type
person for quite a while, and through the years, she has
shown me she has more common sense than most people
and an advanced ability to use rational judgment in cases
of emergency. But in the last four years that I've been
married to this same person (who four years ago became
a grandmother), there have been a time or two I thought
her saddle might be slipping just a bit.

Here lately, she has a tendency to get goofy, especially
when it comes to the grandkids. When I mention this fact,
she seems to get a little ouchy. What I'm trying to say is,
if you think the mother in your wife has made her do some

weird things, just wait till she becomes a grandmother. It's really kind of spooky. It has been my experience that all first-time grandmaws get strange, and they don't get any better as the number of little darlings increases.

When the Little Woman was well over thirty, she became a grandmother, and the first thing she did was to start acting like she was about three and not playing with a full deck.

But I had faith in the Little Woman. I figured it was some kind of stage women go through, and she would come to her senses and everything would get back to normal.

By the time the kid was two, she looked like she might have got her deck filled out, but she just wasn't fishing with all her hooks in the water. By the time the second grandkid arrived, I saw I was married to a complete runaway idiot. The Little Woman had done gone off the deep end.

Don't get me wrong, I kind of like the little varmints, but I'm not to the point of silly over either one of 'em. Just because Joe is the oldest and has more energy than a pasture full of yearling colts doesn't mean I think he's any better than any other kid his age. But he is smart. In fact, he's so smart I'm going to encourage him to pass up all that college education and become a television preacher. If he'll do that, me and him can retire when he's twenty-three, and we can get down to some serious hunting, fishing, and steer roping.

The youngest grandkid is a fine young lady I call "Lonesome." I call her that because she was born on the way to the hospital at the old Hi Lonesome bar. I thought that was a pretty neat trick for a little kid. And now when you see her coming, you just naturally say, "Hi, Lonesome." Ain't that cute?

Back to the Little Woman.

All she can talk about is how precious the little darlings are, and she just didn't have time to fix my supper because she was busy feeding the little critters and learning to speak two-year-old.

When I casually asked why the hell the little darlings' mother couldn't take care of 'em, I stirred up a part of the Little Woman I hadn't seen since the *last* time I had questioned the timing problem concerning my evening meal.

But I have to give her credit for one thing. Her response sure made sense.

She said, "Their mother isn't taking care of them right now because I asked to keep 'em for a little while. I happen to like having them around, and if it's a problem for your eating schedule, fix your own supper."

Now don't get me wrong. I'm not hen-pecked. I just have a world of respect for the Little Woman.

So I stood my ground, agreed with her, and started peeling some potatoes.

Yep, things was starting to get out of hand. The other ladies in the area that hadn't been blessed with any grandkids yet slowly started to visit other people. You know how it works. They don't drop you cold turkey; they just slowly drift away. They started making calls on the county jail and visiting the wine sheds in hopes of finding someone, anyone, who could carry on a conversation that didn't involve a twenty-seven–hour picture program showing the little darlings drooling applesauce down the front of the shirt that when seen in the department store had whispered, "I'm perfect for the kid."

The neighbors have been pretty understanding. It takes a sure-nuff good friend to sit there and listen to some dizzy grandmaw rant and rave about how cute the little bugger was when he stripped off all his clothes at the grocery store and escaped into the vegetable department screaming, "*Oogawawawojo.*" She didn't have any idea what he meant, but she knew it had to be good.

Joe is past four now, and he's showing signs of not making it to five—at least, not if he stays around me very much of the time. I mean, it's tough enough to put the first set of shoes on a colt, but when a noisy little kid comes around the corner of the horse trailer wearing my slicker right when I've got a hind leg picked up, driving a nail becomes an experience that is not all that much fun.

I hate surprises. After I caught my breath, I was going to impress upon his hip pockets how much I really hate surprises. Just because he's little doesn't mean he's stupid.

He shucked the slicker and made the trip to the kitchen in record time. He still doesn't talk all that plain, and I don't know how he got the point across to Grandmaw that quick, but when I finally made it to the kitchen, Grandmaw was waiting.

She wanted to know just *how* I scared the kid so bad and just *why* I would say I was going to wear out a catch rope on his butt when I got my hands on him.

I explained the situation that put his butt on the endangered species list.

The chewing out I got was not minor. I was informed that if I let anything happen to the little darling, I would be able to write a twenty-seven page essay on my new understanding of the meaning of pain. The kid was standing behind Grandmaw the whole time, agreeing with the old silly thing.

I don't care what anybody says, two against one ain't fair. And if one of them two is a grandmaw, it makes it nine against one. Being up against them kind of odds makes the Alamo look like a one-on-one situation.

Grandpaws are a persecuted people.

I told her to keep him out of my way until I at least got the shoes on the colt. Then she could turn him out, and we could start out from scratch. I also mentioned that if she didn't keep him out of my way while I was doing touchy work, I would clean house with the whole bunch of 'em. I'm pretty sure she got the point, even though the door was closed and I was pert near back to the colt when I said it. I didn't have time to make sure because I had a colt to shoe.

Like I said before, Joe hasn't started talking real plain yet, and I have a real hard time trying to understand everything he says.

Grandmaw offered to take the little redheaded one-man demolition derby with us to a roping one Sunday afternoon, and I knew I was in for several hours of animated gibberish with me trying to figure out what was being said. I knew Joe would try and explain. Him and Grandmaw translate for each other.

After an afternoon of trying to win money off a green horse and listening to Grandmaw chew me out, we finally headed home. Seems she didn't think a little kid should be punished for going on with the other kids.

He wasn't going on with 'em. He was leading 'em.

After Larry and me finally got our grandkids out of the water tank in the catch pen, we figured we had better get 'em home before some of the crowd got plumb upset. Larry said we was pretty lucky considering the fact they hadn't tried to hire out as cat cutters yet.

On the way home, the Little Woman decided we had to stop at the grocery store and pick up a few things. This hit Joe just right. He figured since Grandmaw was an easy touch, he could pick up a few things hisself. By the time we got to the store, he had asked for just about everything a kid could ask for, and Grandmaw was getting edgy. When Grandmaw told him he had to stay in the pickup with me, things went to hell right quick.

For a little fellow, he shore made a bunch of racket. I mean, he throwed one snot-slinging, shin-kicking, lung-busting cat-fit. After about thirty seconds of me trying to calm him down, I told him if he did not quit, I was going to give him a better reason to scream than he had at the present. About fifteen seconds later, I gathered him up and we stepped out of the pickup. I wanted plenty of room for my pants-warming hand to move.

Now, when you want to talk about perfect timing, I can be used as perfect example. Just as we got out, there were three little old blue-haired ladies pushing their grocery carts right past the front of my pickup. Joe had drawn the attention of everyone in town who hadn't been buried for more than two weeks, and I was getting some looks from these three old women that would kill a normal person. So I figured if I was going to the pen for child abuse, I might as well draw a life sentence. Just as I was fixing to dust his hip pockets, he decided not only to speak but to speak very *plainly* and very *loud.*

"Oh, Grandpaw," he said, "don't beat me again."

Them three old bats were heading my way. I guess they figured I was the sorriest, meanest SOB since Hitler, and they might figure a way to stop me. This was definitely not a time to show fear.

So, I dusted his pants and chunked him back into the pickup. When I got him in there, I told him if he didn't straighten up, he wouldn't get anything to eat for another two days. At that, I turned and snarled at the blue-haired vigilante committee. They left me alone.

The Little Woman finally showed up and we left. On the way home, it was mentioned I might be a little too rough on the grandkid and I needed to try and understand how it was to be little.

I was understanding, all right. I figured if I lived long enough and he ever tried to hire out as a cat cutter, I was going to do everything in my power to get him put up for adoption.

SEVEN

Female Help:
A Universal Problem

The other day Jim, H.L., and me were sitting around the scale house drinking coffee and discussing the main reasons for all the world's problems. Believe it or not, we were in total agreement on the basic cause of all the really big malfunctions.

It was a unanimous decision.

The trouble with the world, or at least with our little world, was women. It seems like we all had the same problem concerning women, and that problem was that the silly old things just wouldn't listen. It didn't make any difference what you tried to tell 'em, they just didn't pay any attention. When it was all said and done, they just went ahead and did what they wanted to anyway.

Jim commented on the fact that his wife was a pretty good hand a-horseback, but it took him pert near fifteen of their twenty years of blissful marriage to get her trained to the point of doing things right. He did finally get the old thing far enough along that she could go and neighbor without being an embarrassment to him.

I mentioned that I thought he had done a pretty decent job training such a hard-headed person, mainly because in the five years I had known both of them, every time we neighbored, she told him to stay plumb the hell out of the way. I happen to know she can be a little bull-headed about some things, but she is a good hand. Me and her has drug calves together at a branding or two, and I feel that if Jim spent as much time training on her as he said he did, he did an admirable job.

I asked him when he first realized he would have to start the school on doing things the right way, and he told us...

It was right after we got married. Kay was training some young barrel prospects, and she had taken a liking to one of my better colts. I told her she could ride him some but not to get carried away with chasing cans on him, because I didn't want his mind destroyed.

She said he was a good colt, and if he had anything go wrong with his mind, it would be from me chasing all those sick cattle on him. Well, I let that little remark slip on by. After all, she was just a woman.

It was about two weeks after our little talk about the good red colt that I just happened to catch her putting him around the barrels. I came in early from doctoring pasture cattle, and there she was. After I finished telling her how it was going to be, we were in complete agreement on the horse and one or two more subjects. I told her *I* would ride that colt, and *I* would do the training on him, and the training *shore* wouldn't be chasing cans.

She agreed to it, and then she throwed in a little line or two of her own. She said that when I wasn't training on the colt, I could be washing my own clothes and doing my own cooking, and I could do it as long as I kept that self-centered attitude. So after about two days of letting her suffer, I went in and eased her guilty mind. I acted like she was right and told her she could give the red colt some rides, but I would rather she didn't put him on the barrels anymore. End of discussion.

Well, about two months later, we were gathering some yearlings to ship south, and I was riding the good little red colt. He was sure coming along great and starting to really get down and look at a cow. As we were just getting the last few head into the water lot, I noticed the gate on the east end was open. It wasn't any major problem, because it just opened into about an eighty-acre trap, but if the steers got out, we would just have to gather 'em again. I wasn't going to say much about it, because I was the one that had forgot to close the dumb thing. Anyway, I jumped old red out and headed around the water lot in a dead run. I figured I could go around and get the gate closed and come in from the other end. If anyone needed to know why, I could just tell 'em I wanted a better look at what we were going to ship. The first part of that idea wasn't too bad.

In order for me to get around the water lot and to the gate, I had to go through an area that I hated. It was Kay's barrel racing spot, and all them barrels were there.

I never made it to the gate.

As I was helping get Red speeded up, we was fast approaching a barrel. I didn't think about it, 'cause we was going to close a gate. The quickest way to the gate was right past a barrel. That wouldn't be a problem for most folks, you know, running past a barrel.

Well, we got to the barrel, and I kept going toward the gate. I didn't get far though—seems like my aerodynamic body wanted to go to ground rather than stay in the air. About the second or third bounce, I settled down pretty solid, and as I rolled over and sat up, I saw that female-trained colt turn around the second barrel. It seemed to me that someone hadn't listened to a thing I had said. I had started figuring on just what I was going to say and how loud I was going to say it when Kay came whipping by to head off some steers that had found the open gate.

When she came running by, she hollered, "If you're gonna rodeo, you need to either go to town or wait till the work's done." She also asked back over her shoulder who the idiot was that left the gate open.

Looked to me like we was going to war.

As I got up to go catch my horse, he rounded the third barrel and slowed down. When I started in to catch him, he broke and run toward the pens and the other horses. And she thought she could train a barrel horse! Shoot, he never even finished the pattern.

Walking back to the pens, I did a lot of thinking. The way I figured it, it wouldn't do any good to chew her out. It never had done any good so far. Why waste my breath? Besides all that, I didn't want to hurt her feelings by making her cook for just her, so I decided to let things work out by themselves. Maybe she wouldn't say too much about the gate.

H.L. and me could sure understand where he was coming from. Both of us had had our share of wife-training troubles. Old H.L. told him he just about had things figured out about teaching women anything.

"If you want 'em to learn anything at all," he said, "just tell 'em to leave it alone."

H.L. told some sob stories, and to say he had had a tough time of it would be an understatement. He admitted to the fact that after twenty-some-odd years of marriage, he hadn't been able to teach his wife anything. After fifteen years of marriage, he decided to give up and let the poor old cuddly thing just stumble through life the best she could. He told us what made him decide to just give up.

Seems him and his lovely lady, Jan, had taken the car into town to get some scour boluses for some of his baby calves, and then they would get back to the pens and see how things were going...

Well, we got back to the pens just as most of the cows was going back to pasture, but there was three pair that I was wanting to look at still at the water trough. So I closed the gate and walked in to check on the calves. I didn't know what had caused these critters to start scouring so bad, but they sure needed some medicine. I tell Jan to bring me the pills and that old catch rope I keep in the trunk of the car, and I'll just doctor them babies right now while I've got 'em in the pen. She brought everything just like I asked her to, and then she told me to cut the calves off in a smaller pen so the cows wouldn't get excited and I wouldn't have to run the little ones to death trying to get a rope on 'em. Well, the first part of that verbal unleashing of wisdom was okay because I had it in mind anyway, but that little tidbit concerning my roping was not needed and I didn't appreciate it at all.

I told her not to worry about it, just stay out of the way, and when I got a calf down, just bring me a couple of pills. She throwed that box of pills at me and told me she wasn't getting in the pen with those cows after they had been stirred up and especially if any or all of them thought one of their calves was in trouble. I told her if she had any idea as to what she was talking about, it would help, but since she didn't, I would just do it myself. The cows was gentle, I told her, and there wasn't anything to worry about.

I put the pills in my shirt pocket and roped the first calf. The scours hadn't done anything to wear him down, and it was a little harder getting him on the ground than I thought it would be. Fighting off his dear old mama took a little time, but I finally got two pills down him, got the rope off, caught my breath, and headed for the second calf. By this time, all three cows was getting a little edgy, and the calves was acting like their maws. The wife told me to quit being so bull-headed and cut the other two off and doctor 'em separate. I told her since she wasn't in there helping, she could keep quiet and I would do it myself. She got quiet, but I don't think it was because I wanted her to.

The second calf was a little tougher to catch, mainly because all that jabbering the woman had been doing was making him nervous. It took me three loops to catch him. He was a way yonder more active than the first calf, and his mama didn't fight off near as easy. She never actually hit me, but she got so close while I was holding her baby down, she stepped on my ankle and soaked my shirt with some really bad-smelling slobbers. When I finally turned that calf loose, I figured I needed to drink a beer and catch my breath.

As I hobbled over to the fence, I told Jan to get me a beer out of the car. By the time I got to the fence, she hadn't moved. That was when I figured out she was a little upset with me. I told her never mind, I'll just doctor that last calf, and we'll go on to the house. So I hobbled off across the corral after the third calf.

Now, he was considerable bigger than the first two, and a whole lot wilder, and showing a deep desire to be free. There wasn't but about forty-three places in that fence that was weaker than the rest, and it didn't take him long to find one of 'em. He busted through like there wasn't anything there to begin with, and headed north.

The old gal I had been living with got plumb upset. I told her if she hadn't of been hollering so much, that calf wouldn't of got so wild and tore down a fence trying to get away. I also mentioned that now we had to try and catch him so's we could doctor him for the scours *and* see how bad the cut was on his shoulder.

She wanted to know just how I figured I was going to do that since I could barely walk and he seemed to be doing about thirty miles an hour. I told her that if she was half as smart as she thought she was, she would have figured that out.

It was very simple. She would drive the car, and I would ride on the hood. When she got me close enough, I would rope the poor sick critter, and that would be that.

Off we went in hot pursuit. The calf didn't run all that far before he slowed down and started bawling for mama. That made catching up to him pretty easy. I was sitting on the hood, and the little lady eased up pretty close. The calf suspected something and took off again.

I hollered for Jan to speed up. She did. She gassed the car so much it kind of laid me back on the hood, and just about the time I got back up and was fixing to throw a loop, she hit the brakes. I passed that calf on my back and tore up about two hundred yards of perfectly good grass. The calf kept right on going.

When she pulled up to me, I very calmly asked why she decided to stop. She had a sick smile on her face and said she was afraid she was going to run over the poor little thing.

It was about the time I saw that weird grin that I realized I had asked a female-type person who was a little upset with me to drive a car with me on the hood across a pasture chasing a calf, and that this same woman didn't really have any idea as to what she was doing. I got a cold chill. So I explained to her, in the sweetest voice and the softest tone I could muster, just what had to be done. The second time around went somewhat smoother. I got the calf caught with the second loop and was in the process of giving it a couple of pills when all of a sudden it got very dark.

It seems as though during the first chase, the calf was calling for mama and mama was trying to get out to help her baby. I guess during the second chase, somewhere between the first and second loops, maw had got out of the pens and came to the aid of junior. About the time I sat up and looked around, maw and junior was headed off to the draw in the west end of the pasture and Jan was sitting in the car with a silly grin on her face.

After I spit out a dump truck load of dirt and got my breath back, I asked her nice why she didn't warn me about the freight train on legs coming after me. She kept that same silly grin and said she didn't want to holler any more because it might upset the cows and calves, and she sure didn't want to go get 'em any more excited than they already were.

It was right then and there I made up my mind I would never try and do anything like that again. There plain ain't no getting any help with a woman around.

I just sat there and let H.L. and Jim rattle on and on, mainly because I knew just exactly what they were saying. After all, I had tried to teach the Little Woman something about windmills once upon a time.

EIGHT

Head 'Em Up,
Move 'Em Out

All my life, I've had an extremely bad habit of casually getting into trouble. Sometimes I planned it, but most of the time I just happened to be in the wrong place at the wrong time. I have on occasion been the victim of circumstance.

Like the time my wife had taken the pickup and trailer to haul a couple of colts to the vet to have them wormed. I was working at a feed yard and keeping my horses in the company pen. I tried keeping them in the backyard at home, but the neighbors seemed to think they attracted flies.

The Little Woman drove her car to the feed yard and took my rig. Since I had made arrangements to leave the horses at a friend's place for the night, I would just bring her car home when I got off work.

Most people would think such an everyday sort of agreement is okay, and I'm sure that for most people, it is. When you're trying to get ahead in the calf trading world, though, it could be dangerous.

Just before quitting time, a friend of mine who owned a small farm just west of the yards stopped by and asked if I wanted a couple of dogied calves. Lightning had hit his pens the night before and killed his nurse cow, two calves, twelve peacocks, and a banty hen. He was a little disgusted with the way things was going and figured on getting plumb out of the cow business. He told me he would give 'em to me if I would come by and pick 'em up that afternoon.

I accepted right quick. After he drove off, I got to wondering how I was gonna get them calves the twenty-two miles to my place without a pickup or trailer.

I tried to con a couple of cowboys into hauling 'em home for me, but they wouldn't. It seemed they were going to a jackpot cutting at Bovina, and they just didn't have time to make a round trip to Texico before all the cutting and slashing got started.

Being the type not to let little things like not having my pickup stand in my way, I just figured I'd throw a couple of feed sacks in the back seat, stuff the calves in, and haul 'em home. Of course, what I was gonna do with the little critters when I got 'em home hadn't even crossed my mind yet.

When I got to Oscar's place that evening, I could see why he might have been a little upset at the cow business. He not only lost most of his cow herd with one quick stroke of lightning, but he lost his new cowshed and all the new lumber he had used to build his pens with. When the lightning hit, it burnt down everything it didn't make toothpicks out of.

Now these two calves he gave me were still pretty addled, but they looked good out of their eyes, and their ankles didn't pop when they walked. He had fed 'em out of a bottle twice that day, and they seemed to be on their way to recovery for the time being.

Oscar wasn't a dummy by any means, and he was generally pretty helpful, but today he wasn't gonna help at all. He said after the second feeding, he was through with cattle forever. And since he had given 'em to me, they were all mine and to get 'em off his place. He handed me a bill of sale and headed to the house.

Since I was in the Little Woman's car, I didn't have a rope with me. So I just used my belt and led one calf to the car.

Like I mentioned before, the calves were still a little addled, and I had very little trouble loading the first one. Notice I said very little trouble. It's not all that easy to stuff a two hundred pound crossbred calf into the backseat of a two-door 1965 Pontiac Tempest. I didn't figure the rip in the seat on the passenger's side would show up all that much.

I finally got the little linebred, hammer-headed, burnt-hair–smelling idiot down in the floor and went back to get the other one.

It's really amazing to me how much healing power a little rough treatment can have on a survivor of an electrical storm.

By the time I got the other critter to the car, the first one seemed to be fully revived, but just a tad upset.

When I opened the door to put calf number two in the back seat, I was greeted by a calf that must have had a touch of claustrophobia. I'm just guessing of course, but he sure acted like he wanted out of the car.

He got out of the car.

But me being the quick and active type of feller I am, I managed to trap him by a front foot. It's a tricky thing to hold on to a belt attached to an addled calf and keep the wide-awake calf's front foot stuck down the front of your shirt while at the same time maneuvering both of them into the back seat of a two-door Pontiac.

Oscar came to the rescue just in time.

He grabbed the escapee, stuffed him back in the car, and held him there while I crammed the other one in. He said the only reason he came to help was if he helped he would get rid of 'em quicker. Then he gave me the feed buckets and said goodbye one more time.

I took the hint, said thank you, got in the car, and headed for Texico.

Loading the calves was easy compared to hauling 'em. I made it to the first curve just east of Farwell, and the cattle-hauling business went to hell.

I guess all the calf manna and instant milk they'd been fed, along with their complete recovery from the electrical shock and just a touch of road sickness, made the little critters restless.

Both of 'em got up out of the floor at the same time.

The Bramer cross decided the only thing to calm him down would be to drive. The Hereford figured since the other one was gonna drive, he would keep a watch out the back window in case anybody tried to sneak up on us.

I don't mind telling you, it isn't all that easy to avoid oncoming traffic when you're fighting off an overbearing calf. We were coming to a deep curve with a Texas highway cop in it slowing things up.

I saw the cop just in time to swerve and pass him on the right. He noticed I was in trouble and flashed on his lights right quick and started trying to clear the way for me.

The crossbred calf figured he was after us and started taking evasive action. He dove down to the gas pedal. It's spooky when two hundred pounds of beef lays down on your foot and the gas pedal at the same time.

The old bull wagon gained some speed.

I guess the sudden burst of speed and all those flashing lights kinda upset the little Hereford's tummy. As I was trying to get that dern crossbred off my foot, brake the car, and stay on the highway, I felt a blanket of rather strong-smelling wet warmth settle across my shoulders.

Boy, was I in trouble. I could see me sleeping in that car with two dogie calves for the rest of my life. Yep, the Little Woman was gonna be some upset.

After I stood there smelling like calf manna and used instant milk and explained for a while, the Texas highway cop finally went back to his car laughing. I figured the state could build thirty miles of new road with what they were gonna make off the tickets I just got.

Now for the hard part.

Up to this point, I hadn't thought much about where I was gonna put those calves. All at once, it occurred to me that if I couldn't keep horses in the backyard, the neighbors sure weren't gonna let me keep calves.

I resorted to devious thinking.

If I could sneak the critters into the house and stash 'em in the bathroom for the night, I could take 'em to the sale in Clovis the next day. I figured I might get enough out of 'em to pay for the tickets and getting the car cleaned.

I am a firm believer that no matter how much bad luck you have, it can't last forever. On that day, I happened to be right. The Little Woman hadn't got home yet, and the goofy neighbors weren't out standing on their porches.

I got both calves stashed in the bathroom, cleaned myself up, and went to work on the car.

I only had about eight dollars in cash, but I decided to take the car to Clovis and use one of those car-wash places for the really nasty spots.

Me being the thoughtful husband most women wish for, I left the Little Woman a note. "Sheila, don't get too upset with our new pets. I'll be back in a few minutes. Lots of love. Me."

I figured that would keep her calmed down till I could get home and explain. It didn't.

I got back from the car wash about 9:30, and the car was pert near spotless. There were only a few spots that would not come plumb clean, and I had patched a couple of small rips with some of that real pretty silver tape. I wasn't too worried about the rips, because the Little Woman never rode in the back seat anyway.

When I walked into the house, I detected a bit of hostility in the air. I tried to be calm and show complete control. I waltzed into the kitchen and asked cheerfully, "What's for supper?"

I got hit in the chest with a feed sack that was not only soggy but smelled terrible.

"You want supper? You fix it. You can fix your new pets the same thing you fix yourself. And when you get done fixin' supper, you can fix the bathroom. We now have a long-eared black calf that's wearing a toilet seat and a Hereford calf that's repainting the whole room. I don't care where you put 'em, but they better be outa here in under an hour, and you have ten minutes more than that to get the mess cleaned up." With that, she stormed off into the bedroom and slammed the door.

I figured since the state of the bathroom was my fault, and I wasn't really all that hungry, I would just go ahead and clean up the mess.

What saved me was the Little Woman had brought the horse trailer home with her. That's where the calves spent the night. I finished cleaning the bathroom about three in the morning. I still haven't figured out how two critters that short could repaint the ceiling.

Since I was off the next day, I took the troublemaking demons to the sale. This time I used the pickup and trailer.

To this day, I'll never know why the Little Woman got into the back seat of the car. I guess it doesn't really matter, because I made enough off the calves to pay for my traffic tickets and only owe $33.12 on the new upholstery job.

I'm not gonna say I wouldn't take any more calves if someone gave 'em to me, but I am saying you can bet your last dollar I won't haul 'em in the Little Woman's car or board 'em in the bathroom.

Roping Can Be Hazardous To Your Health

*A*s we grow older, we develop a kind of seventh sense. It's called caution. Unlike the other six, which stay pretty active, it just sits there in the back of our minds.

For some, this sense comes early in life, and for others, it comes later because those others are slow to realize how important a little caution can be.

Caution means thinking.

Thinking means being a little distracted from the activity that requires caution.

So, as I see it, caution is the main reason a lot of things don't get done.

Still, if it wasn't for lack of caution, America's youth would be even worse educated than they are now. I know for a fact that me not using caution a time or two in my young life produced some fairly violent forms of education—but it *was* education.

Like the time Dear Old Dad gave me my first new rope.

I was in the sixth grade, and until that time of my life, the only ropes I ever had were pretty well wore out and maybe even spliced a time or two.

Dear Old Dad was tired of me asking for a new rope, so we went down to the saddle house and he cut off a length of Plymouth Silk Manila from the coil. He built me my own personal catch rope.

I'll never forget his instructions when he gave it to me: "That rope is not a toy. Never, I mean never, put it on anything you can't get it off of by yourself."

I knew Dear Old Dad was pretty smart, but he was wrong about that rope not being a toy. I had seen him and them other guys playing with ropes ever since I could remember. There's no telling how many stray steers and cows had been roped, tripped, and tied just for the heck of it, or forefooted just so's the boys could stay in practice.

But I agreed with the old cuddly thing anyway, took my new non-toy, and went merrily off to find something not to play with.

About an hour later, Dear Old Dad and a couple of hands were out in the pasture doing something that was probably important, and Dear Old Mom was in the house doing her Mom-thing with my kid sister, and I was closing the gate on a big black crossbred Bramer cow. I don't have any idea why she came in to water by herself, but I sure did appreciate it.

There's something that I might mention about tying off: unless you are a-horseback, don't. And that's where caution—or rather the lack thereof—enters this story.

I slipped the horn knot over my right wrist and proceeded to sneak up on old snake. I used the horn knot because I didn't want to have to chase my rope down or take a chance on it getting drug around the corral and frayed to threads in all those rocks. Being in the sixth grade didn't mean I was stupid.

Well, I learned pretty sudden-like that it's pert near impossible to rope a cow when she's blowing snot in your hip pockets.

But I made up my mind that I was going to rope this ill-trained old bat. I just hadn't figured out how. About the third time she put me on top of the fence, I figured it out.

I slipped the horn knot off my wrist and put it over the top of a fence post. Then I managed to make the old thing so mad she tried to climb on top with me. She would run at the fence, stick her head up, and blow slobbers all over me, then turn and run towards the middle of the pen.

After three really bad throws, I finally caught her.

I kinda missed my slack a little, and the loop fit her like a workhorse collar. It was about the time she jerked the fence out from under me and the top half of that post hit her right square in the tail that I remembered the part of Dear Old Dad's advice about not putting a rope on anything that I couldn't get it off of by myself.

If it hadn't of been for a neighbor coming over to borrow some kind of tool, I guess I'd still be out there trying to get my rope back. He felt sorry for me, and he not only got my rope back, he even got the fence tied up and did away with the post.

He said he wouldn't tell Dear Old Dad if I promised not to do anything that stupid again, and of course I agreed.

The neighbor got the tools he'd come for, and I took my rope and went to find something else to do for awhile.

It seems that I still had not discovered the true meaning of the phrase "don't put your rope on anything you can't take it off of."

A few days later, some neighbors were over one evening to visit and drink coffee. I had just managed to put a new hondo in my not-so-new catch rope, and since it was dark, I was in the house trying to mind my own business when it happened.

It was one of the few times my kid sister and me was getting along. I had been practicing my forefooting loop on her. She would come down the hall and into the living room, and I would try and catch her feet as she went by. It was a friendly game. I wasn't trying to stack her up or anything like that. We were just playing.

Then she done it.

She grabbed my rope and managed to get a knot tied in it that has never been identified in the Boy Scout handbook or any known sailor's manual. Then she ran back into the kitchen.

Of course, you know, that meant war.

Well, I finally got the knot out of my old whaleline and waited for the untrustworthy little snot to come back down the hall so's I could forefoot her and jerk her down on her little rotten head.

Up till now, I haven't said much about Dear Old Mom. It's not that I'm trying to shun her; it's just that I always got along pretty good with the old gal. She never was one to get into the problems of me being the type to kinda mess things up on occasion. She had voiced her opinion about the way Dear Old Dad had more or less let me have my head (so to speak), and, I might add, she was seriously opposed to me having a rope of any kind—especially in the house.

Still, she tolerated the rope and didn't really say all that much even when I had to have a little help turning one of the dogs loose. She just wasn't crazy about me packing a rope around all the time, and the only reason I had it in the house then was because I was trying to get a new hondo in it.

I had total revenge on my mind and my sights set for the first set of legs that come through that hall and into the living room. Timing never has been my best suit.

Bet you can't guess who was the first one through the door.

I'll give you a hint: whoever it was was carrying a tray with a pot of coffee and about sixty-five cups to drink it out of.

I never knew coffee cups could shatter so loud and in so many pieces, and I didn't know a man screamed quite like that when he had hot coffee poured in his lap. But they can and he did.

I had done it. I had forefooted Dear Old Mom.

For a couple of seconds, Dear Old Dad thought Dear Old Mom had just tripped and managed to throw the coffee over the back of the couch onto him, but when Dear Old Mom came up off the floor with my rope in her hand I think Dear Old Dad may have guessed what really happened.

The neighbors were somewhat confused. They didn't know whether to show concern about the woman on the floor or laugh at the man peeling down to his underwear as fast as he could.

I personally didn't care about their dilemma. I was trying to figure out how to escape through one of the two doors to the house, each of which by now was blocked by an adult I knew for a fact to be a little upset, one with a rope in her hand and the other one with bright pink thighs.

There was no escape.

Dear Old Mom grabbed me and took me and my rope into the kitchen. She made me sit and watch her cut that rope into pieces about six inches long—except for the last piece. That one she left about four foot long and proceeded to double it.

Being in the sixth grade didn't mean I was ignorant. I knew what was fixing to happen.

And it did.

When she got through with me, I headed for my bedroom. All the adults in the living room was handing me with some pretty hard looks. Dear Old Dad was just getting back from putting on some cooler and dryer clothes.

As I started to go past him, he said to me. "I told you not to put that rope on anything you couldn't get it off of."

It was two days later that I tried to get a letter sent off to the *Tucumcari Tribune* wanting to place an ad for the adoption of one little girl, semihousebroke, with outstanding knot-tying abilities. But that's another story.

Messing-Up Lessons

Very few people understand how hard life is for a young man that wants to do right, but just can't seem to get it together.

I learned early it didn't make any difference what it was you were trying to do. If it failed, you'd be in a mess of trouble with the older people that hung around just so they could catch you messing up.

For this reason, I have always been one to try and do it right the first time.

Not many people know that, because most have seen me mess things up the first time. And usually they'd be so disgusted they'd leave before I could make the proper apologies or quit bawling long enough to straighten out the mess I caused.

The schooling I got concerning mess-ups has carried over into my adult life. I'm not saying I don't mess things up anymore; I'm just saying it's harder to catch me at it.

Once when I was just a kid, I tried to talk my little sister into parachuting out of the barn loft. I had snuck a pillow-case from the hall closet and with the help of my pert-near perfect memory—(I'd seen a picture of a parachute somewhere one time)—I used plenty of binder twine and old harness leather to make one.

The thing was, I needed a test jumper.

It wasn't that I was afraid to use it myself. But, see, as the parachute designer, I needed to watch it work so I could build another one, and both of us could jump at the same time later.

It didn't work all that well.

It must've been the way I had it packed down the back of my kid sister's pants. By the time I managed to get her throwed out the barn loft door (jumping conditions protested somewhat by the test jumper), I realized I was standing in the barn loft with the rip cord still in my hand. I was also pretty well scratched up.

Back a few minutes earlier, when I was in the process of convincing my kid sister to jump for the glory of the free world, I failed to notice that Dear Old Dad had backed the pickup into the barn for some unknown reason. All that was sticking out was the cab.

Anyway, the chute didn't open, and my timing was as awful as usual. Baby Sister hit the cab of that pickup just about the same time Dear Old Dad was getting ready to get out.

I knew right away something was wrong. I had jumped out of that barn loft several times, and when I hit the ground, it never sounded quite like the roof of the chicken house caving in.

I guess it spooked Dear Old Dad, 'cause he pert near ripped his head off trying to get out of the pickup without opening the door.

I figure it was all that parachute in the seat of her pants that saved her. It was probably the padding that caused her to bounce off the top of the cab onto the hood and then roll off on the ground and skin her nose.

She was the lucky one. All she got was a skint nose.

Dear Old Dad got a really big knot on his head, and I got my sitter broke. I couldn't sit down for the better part of a week. But I learned my lesson. Actually I learned a couple of lessons. One was you don't pack parachutes down pants, and the other was you make sure there ain't no pickups in the way when you test a parachute.

Like I said, I've learned a lot about messing up. I have also learned that when I'm going to do something that might be considered controversial, I need to do it when there isn't anybody else around.

Kind of like the other day when it was just me and my grandson, Joe at the house.

Joe is in the second grade, and in spite of taking after his Mammy (his grandmaw, the Little Woman) in his ungodly talent for messing things up, he is a pretty good kid. To my knowledge, he isn't afraid of anything except me, and that's only when I'm riled.

We had spent the afternoon with him working the roping chutes for me, and after a quick soda pop at the house, we went out to do the chores and look over the roping steers.

Joe had told me he would like to be a bull rider. (That statement clinched my argument that he took after his Mammy.) Me being the type not to mouth off, I didn't discourage him—but I didn't really encourage him either.

The situation was this. We was in the steer pen, and he mentioned again his desire to be an ox jobber, and I figured, why not? I had a big blue-roan steer that was pretty gentle and easy to get around, so I thought he might just let the kid sit on him. I grabbed the steer by one horn, and with my free hand, I put Joe on top. Well, the steer side-stepped a time or two and then just started walking around the steer pen with what looked like might be a future champion on his back.

I guess I got a little carried away with Joe's excitement. He was doing so good, I asked him if he thought he could rear back and stab that old steer.

Joe said he could.

I said, "Well, do it."

I had never seen a little kid get throwed quite that high before.

I tried to catch him before he hit the ground, but me being the slim, trim, athletic figure I am, I was just a tad late. When I got to him his eyes was still kinda rolling around and he wasn't real sure what had happened. I checked him out real close, and I asked him if he was all right.

I had him up facing me and, over my shoulder, the house. He was having a little trouble standing up. When I asked him one more time if he was all right, he managed to give me an answer which made me realize I had better do something before Mammy got home.

What he said was, "No, Pawpaw, I'm not hungry. You can have the last bite."

I thought a cloud had covered the sun, but it turned out that Mammy was already home and looming up fast.

She was fixing to hurt me permanent 'cause I had got her precious grandson bucked off. She was talking bad to me, and I'm not one to just stand there and take a lot of unnecessary verbal abuse from anyone. At least I didn't used to be.

I told her he wasn't hurt and just leave us alone and I'd take care of him.

Bad move.

Mammy gathered him up and headed for the house and was making a terrible fuss over him. He was tough, and he wasn't crying, but the little redheaded traitor was agreeing with her.

That was the day I made up my mind never to do anything ever again unless I was by myself.

I'm not sure if what Joe said just before they went into the house helped me or not, but at least he was thinking about me.

"That's okay, Mammy," he said. " He won't get me killed on purpose."

ELEVEN

The Trouble with Heroes

Just the other day, I had a small discussion with my grandson about how important it is for him to think ahead a little bit. I tried to impress upon his mind by way of his hip pockets that when Grandpaw was shoeing a horse, it wasn't polite to jump off the back of the pickup swinging a big stick and singing the theme song from some goofy turtle show.

After I had warmed up his britches and things had settled down, I explained that even though it was fun for him to be acting like a turtle, it wasn't all that much fun for me to hobble around on the swelled leg and ankle I got from him causing the colt to try to kick me and him both plumb out of the county.

Grandmaw rescued the little darling, and I got back to trying to get shoes on the colt. I figured I would smoke a cigarette and let the colt stand tied for a few minutes to calm down. All this got me to doing a little thinking.

I've always been one to stop and think things out pretty good before I tried anything that might be a little dangerous. Only on rare occasions did I just charge and not worry about the outcome.

Like the time I was in the fourth grade. Getting to go to town was a pretty big deal, and I generally got to go to the movies. One particular movie I saw was a Tarzan film.

Now, old Tarzan was a pretty good hand at saving the women and the elephants and whatever else was in trouble. He could kill a lion bare-handed and never get much of a scratch. I liked this old boy's style, and when I seen him swinging from tree to tree on them vines, I decided that was a pert near perfect way to travel. But when he jumped off that twenty-thousand-foot-high bluff (I was only in the fourth grade, and when you're just over three-foot tall, things look higher) into that little old river, I knew the man was going to be my hero.

There was a problem or two, though. Where we lived, there wasn't any trees to swing from. All the trees around our place was short and had thorns on 'em. We sure didn't have any lions to kill by hand, so I tried to save an imaginary woman explorer from the deadly clutches of a big old tom cat gone mad. (He might not have been to start with, but by the time he got me turned loose, he was definitely mad. I figured the next time I saw Tarzan, I would pay a little more attention to how he handled that big old lion.)

Since rescuing women explorers was out, I thought I'd try and perfect the dive-into-the-river-from-the-cliff trick. We didn't have a river either, but me being the thinking-type kid that I was, I would pretend that our six-foot-deep and thirty-foot-across storage tank was a flowing river and the thirty-foot-high windmill tower was a cliff. The tank had water in it, which was good, but it only had about three feet of water in it, which I failed to notice.

I got situated on the platform of that old windmill, and I was thinking pretty serious about just climbing down and forgetting the Tarzan thing when the wind changed.

I put my original plan in motion. When I saw the wheel coming around on the changing wind and fixing to knock me off, I jumped.

I hit the water and the cement bottom in very rapid succession, having picked up a lot of momentum going down. Somehow I managed to hit at an angle, and I guess that's what saved me—if you can call it "saved." I slid across the bottom of that water tank so fast it not only peeled the hide off my face, it shredded the fronts of my shirt and levis, and dragged the toes plumb out of my next-to-new Keds.

Dear Old Dad had seen me take the jump. He was driving in from the west pasture, and I guess it scared him pretty bad. He jumped into the tank about the same time I ricocheted off the far side of my river.

I was bawling so hard from my self-inflicted skinning that he didn't whip me, but the chewing out I got was world-class.

Among other things, he wanted to know why I had done such a stupid thing.

I said I figured if Tarzan could do it, I could too. (I didn't mention trying to save the lady from the midget lion.)

After Dear Old Dad had calmed down a little, he very carefully asked if I had even considered the fact that Tarzan could swim and I couldn't. Or the fact that the river probably had a little more than three feet of water in it.

Well, that was a lesson learned, and I never forgot it for at least two or three weeks. And I did some serious studying on other candidates for the position of hero.

It wasn't that I didn't already have a couple of heroes; I just thought I needed someone besides Roy Rogers and Gene Autry to look up to. It always amazed me how those two could almost whip a whole gang of outlaws and then get knocked out. Course the outlaws knew when they woke up, they'd be plumb mad, so the bad guys would head for the hills. The big fight scene would almost always happen in the bad guys' boss's office upstairs from the local bar, and the bad guys would run downstairs, get their horses, and head for the hills.

The hero would wake up and realize the bad guys were getting away, and in order to save time, he'd climb out the window (which just happened to be above the exact spot where his horse was tied), jump off the balcony onto his horse, and get after the villains.

Well, one morning I was up in the barn loft practicing my bar room brawling when some sneaking, low-life, dirty, double-crossing snake hit me across the back with a chair. As I was laying there waiting for the bad guys to get a decent head start, I heard a horse come up to the barn.

I looked out the loft door just in time to see Dear Old Dad step off, drop the reins, and walk inside.

For once, my timing was perfect.

Here was my chance to maybe catch some bad guys and impress Dear Old Dad with how I could get on a horse from anywhere.

About halfway down, I realized the horse I was jumping on wasn't a normal horse. It was Old Spooks.

And I guess the change in altitude had kinda messed up my ability to judge distance properly. I hit him right square on the hips.

The last thing I saw for a while was the top of the barn hallway as Old Spooks pulled a one-horse stampeding idiot fit.

We both went into the barn with Dear Old Dad, but only Old Spooks came out.

I was waking up as Dear Old Dad was trying to explain to Mom what had happened. "I guess the kid walked up and scared that horse, 'cause when I came out of the saddle room, I got run over by a bellerin' freight train. And just as I was getting up and trying to get out of the way, that silly son of a buck run over me on his way back out. I don't think the boy's hurt, but I bet he thinks twice before he walks up behind another horse."

I just laid there with my ice pack and two black eyes and figured what Dear Old Dad didn't know wouldn't hurt me anymore.

This trying to be a hero ain't all it's cracked up to be.

Just before school got started that year, I made it to another movie and found not just a hero but a way of doing things that looked a lot safer than what I'd been trying.

This new hero was a space-type fellow, and he had a ray gun that could dry up rivers and make things disappear. He had a gas pack on his back some of the time which meant he could fly without the use of an airplane. With that kind of equipment, he didn't have to depend on vines or horses. Instead of diving off cliffs, he could just gas hisself over the river—or dry it up and walk across.

This was my kind of guy. (I had been using an old water pistol as a ray gun, and Dear Old Dad never even knew when I zapped him.) Pretty slick kind of operation, I thought.

Then came fall shipping.

We were shipping about six truckloads of steers out one weekend, and Dear Old Dad had given me the job of helping the steers up that chute. Most would go pretty good, but every once in awhile one of the black Bramer cross steers would show his true colors and get nasty.

Dear Old Dad had made a hot shot out of a walking cane, electric wire, two beer can openers, and a battery with some kind of coil off a T-model Ford. When he got it all put together and had everything taped just right, it weighed about four hundred pounds and could kill flies at ten feet. The sucker shot a blue flame and crackled every time you pushed the little button.

I thought it was pretty darn neat.

Dear Old Dad had given me a real job that very few could do properly and had supplied me with a ray gun that made that space cadet look like a piker.

The loading chute was solid boards on the outside so the cattle couldn't see out, and there was a catwalk all the way from the back of the crowding pen to the front of the loading chute.

When I heard the gate close on the crowding pen, I would stand up, lean over, and holler at the steers. The walk was a little too low for me to get a good reach, but I managed to zap a couple of stragglers. I soon found out if I timed it just right, I could zap one and load ten. That hot shot was hot.

The day had started out hot and dusty, and then the wind started blowing. You couldn't see more than ten or fifteen feet. Things slowed down considerable.

The next to the last truck was backing up to the chute. It was about ten feet away when it broke down. The truckers told Dear Old Dad and the other cowboys it would be about forty-five minutes before they would have it fixed.

While everyone was trying to smoke and visit a little and ignore the wind all at the same time, I was busy trying to catch the corrals on fire and fry flies with my new special-designed ray gun.

I was just about to get bored with the limited reach of the blue flame when I seen it. I had tried the ray gun out on everything except drying up rivers, and here was my chance!

It wasn't until about two days after the wreck (when I could actually sit down at the dinner table again) that I made up my mind to think ahead a litle bit about what could possibly go wrong before I just jumped in and did something.

See, I was standing there minding my own business when I saw a puddle of water forming at the bottom of that solid board fence.

Yep, I did it. I tried to dry up the river.

I didn't actually dry it up, but I'll guarantee you one thing: I stopped the flow.

I've never heard a man scream like that before or since.

I dropped the ray gun and left out.

The hands couldn't find out what happened because Dear Old Dad couldn't tell 'em. He just laid there shaking and muttering something about lightning and never going to the bathroom again unless he was in the house. Then one of the neighbors noticed my ray gun and that I wasn't with it.

After the discussion we had when Dear Old Dad found me, I swore off movies. And I flat out gave up the idea of ever having a hero that was worth a plugged nickel.